Veterans Day

By Amanda Doering Tourville
Illustrated by Todd Ouren

Content Consultant:
Richard Jensen, Ph.D.
Author, Scholar, and Historian

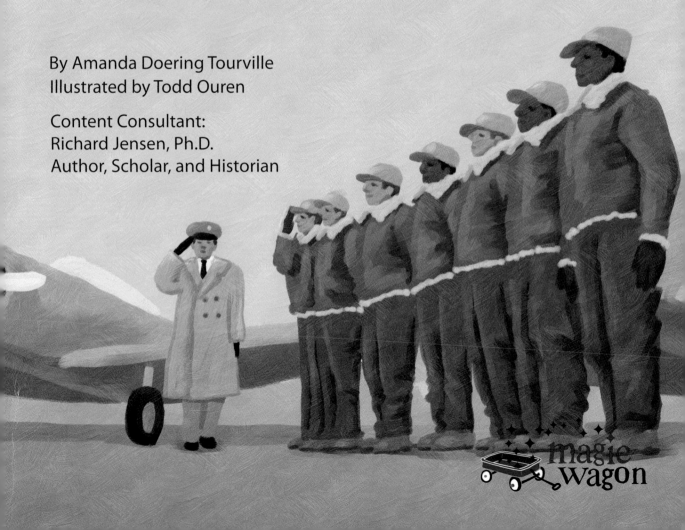

magic Wagon

Visit us at www.abdopublishing.com

Published by Magic Wagon, a division of the ABDO Publishing Group, 8000 West 78th Street, Edina, Minnesota, 55439. Copyright © 2008 by Abdo Consulting Group, Inc. International copyrights reserved in all countries. All rights reserved. No part of this book may be reproduced in any form without written permission from the publisher. Looking Glass Library™ is a trademark and logo of Magic Wagon.

Printed in the United States.

Text by Amanda Doering Tourville
Illustrations by Todd Ouren
Edited by Patricia Stockland
Interior layout and design by Nicole Brecke
Cover design by Nicole Brecke

Library of Congress Cataloging-in-Publication Data
Doering Tourville, Amanda, 1980—
 Veterans Day / Amanda Doering Tourville ; illustrated by Todd Ouren.
    p. cm. — (Our nation's pride)
 Includes index.
 ISBN 978-1-60270-117-5
 1. Veterans Day—Juvenile literature. 2. Holidays—Juvenile literature. I. Ouren, Todd. II. Title.
D671.D64 2008
394.264—dc22
                    2007034078

Table of Contents

Honoring the People Who Serve

It is November 11, and your city is celebrating.

You go to a parade. People in many different

uniforms walk by. Bands play patriotic music.

A man on a horse carries a large American flag.

You are celebrating Veterans Day. We celebrate

Veterans Day to honor people who have served in

the U.S. military.

5

The Great War

Between 1914 and 1918, many countries were at war. At the time, the war was called the Great War. It is now known as World War I. The United States entered the war in 1917. On November 11, 1918, Germany surrendered and agreed to stop fighting.

This day became known as Armistice Day.

The End of Fighting

When people heard that the countries had

stopped fighting, there was a great celebration.

All over the world, people gathered in the

streets. Businesses closed so that everyone

could join in the fun. People in every country

were happy that the fighting had ended.

The First Anniversary

On November 11, 1919, President Woodrow

Wilson made a statement. He said that the

United States would celebrate the first anniversary

of Armistice Day. The country was to remember

Armistice Day with parades and meetings. All

business should stop for two minutes at 11:00 a.m.

Other Countries Remember

The United States was not the only country to remember Armistice Day. In 1920, Great Britain and France honored those who died in the war. Each country created a tomb for one soldier who had died. No one knew who these soldiers were. They stood for all the unknown people who had died for their countries.

13

Tomb of the Unknown Soldier

In 1921, the United States also created a tomb for one unknown soldier. At 11:00 a.m. on November 11, 1921, the soldier was lowered into the marble tomb. This was the third anniversary of Armistice Day. The nation fell silent to honor the unknown soldier.

A Federal Holiday

In the 1920s and 1930s, many states passed laws to make Armistice Day a state holiday. In 1938, lawmakers made Armistice Day a legal federal holiday. It was to be celebrated every November 11. On this day, the nation would remember the people who fought and died in World War I.

World War II and the Korean War

After World War I, most people did not think there would ever be another large war. They were wrong. In 1939, World War II began. The United States entered the war in 1941. The war ended in 1945. Americans also fought in the Korean War. This war was fought from 1950 to 1953.

Armistice Day
Becomes Veterans Day

Many Americans fought in World War II and

the Korean War. The country agreed that these

people needed to be honored, too. In 1954,

President Dwight D. Eisenhower changed the

name of Armistice Day. The holiday was renamed

Veterans Day.

People wanted Veterans Day to honor those who had served the nation. They also wanted to remember veterans who had been killed or wounded. Veterans Day remembers all of these brave people.

Celebrating Veterans Day

We celebrate Veterans Day to honor the people who have served in the U.S. military. Some veterans have fought in wars. Some people are still fighting. On November 11, we show that we are grateful to veterans for protecting our country.

Veterans Day is celebrated in different ways.

Churches hold special services to honor veterans.

Many towns and cities have parades. Some people

visit cemeteries where veterans are buried. Some

schools and businesses have the day off. Students

who have school might write letters to people

serving in the military. Schools may invite veterans

to talk to the students.

Visiting a cemetery or a memorial shows

respect to military people and their loved ones.

The United States celebrates Veterans Day

to honor everyone who has served in the military.

We remember the people who protected our

country. We thank the people who still serve in

the military.

Fun Facts

• Veterans Day and Memorial Day are similar holidays. But they honor veterans in different ways. On Memorial Day, we honor people who died in wars. On Veterans Day, we honor everyone who has served or is serving in the military.

• Australia, Canada, and Great Britain call this holiday Remembrance Day.

• Each year at Arlington National Cemetery, the president and high-ranking military officials speak. Military bands play patriotic music. The president lays a wreath of flowers at the Tomb of the Unknown Soldier.

• There are several organizations that veterans can join. Some of these include the Veterans of Foreign Wars (VFW), the Disabled American Veterans (DAV), the American Legion, and the National Association for Black Veterans.

Glossary

anniversary—a date marking an important event.

armistice—an agreement to stop fighting.

lawmakers—people who make laws.

military—the armed forces that protect a country. The five branches of the U.S. military are Air Force, Army, Coast Guard, Navy, and Marines.

patriotic—showing love for one's country.

surrender—to give up; to stop fighting an enemy.

tomb—an aboveground burial chamber.

uniform—a set of clothing worn by everyone in a certain group.

veteran—a person who has served in the military.

On the Web

To learn more about Veterans Day, visit ABDO Publishing Company on the World Wide Web at **www.abdopublishing.com**. Web sites about Veterans Day are featured on our Book Links page. These links are routinely monitored and updated to provide the most current information available.

Index